A Perfect Pancake Cookbook

First published in Great Britain in
2026 by Hamlyn, an imprint of
Octopus Publishing Group Ltd
Carmelite House
50 Victoria Embankment
London EC4Y 0DZ
www.octopusbooks.co.uk

An Hachette UK Company
www.hachette.co.uk

The authorized representative in the EEA
is Hachette Ireland, 8 Castlecourt Centre,
Dublin 15, D15 XTP3, Ireland
(email: info@hbgi.ie)

Distributed in the US by
Hachette Book Group
1290 Avenue of the Americas,
4th and 5th Floors,
New York, NY 10104

Distributed in Canada by
Canadian Manda Group,
664 Annette St.,
Toronto, Ontario,
Canada M6S 2C8

ISBN 978-0-6006-3986-2
eISBN 978-0-6006-3988-6

A CIP catalogue record for this book is available from the British Library.

Printed and bound in China.

10 9 8 7 6 5 4 3 2 1

Publisher: Lucy Pessell
Designers: Isobel Platt & Kath Anderson
Editor: Tim Leng
Assistant Editor: Samina Rahman
Production Controller:
Lucy Carter & Nic Jones

Picture Acknowledgements iStock: a_namenko 4, ALLEKO 61, bhofack2 46, Elizaveta Bauer 23, gollykim 77, gorchittza2012 67, Liudmyla Chuhunova 69, los_angela 18, manyakotic 35, Nuclear_lily 8, PeteerS 64, vaaseenaa 21, zeljkosantrac 32; Octopus Publishing Group: 11, 13, 31, 43, 45, 49, 51, 59.

This FSC® label means that materials used for the product have been responsibly sourced.

A Perfect Pancake Cookbook

Recipes for irresistible pancakes, churros, waffles and more

Eloise Goode

hamlyn

CONTENTS

Pancake, crêpe, griddle cake, flapjack, Johnnycake, blintz, blini, pikelet, hotcake...whatever you call them, these batter-based treats hold a special place in the hearts of many. In fact, pancakes are eaten and celebrated all over the world – from the familiar fluffy stack smothered in maple syrup to the sweetly stuffed Hotteok from South Korea and wobbly, souffléd ones from Japan. The beauty of pancakes is their versatility – they can be enjoyed at any time of day, and the sky's the limit when it comes to flavours: you can add ingredients to the batter, load them with as many toppings as you like and drizzle them in sauces – the possibilities are endless.

Within these pages you'll find a delectable collection of mouthwatering recipes that take you beyond the humble pancake and its classic lemon and sugar topping. Allow mealtimes to become a celebration with American-style pancakes; serve them stacked high, accompanied by bacon or fruit, and topped with a heavy hand of maple syrup. Perhaps an elegant crêpe Suzette is more your style? And if you fancy something a little different, there are a selection of recipes that use batter in other wonderful ways.

So, gather your bowls and whisk, roll up your sleeves and begin with a Vanilla Maple Latte – it's time to rise and pancake! Embrace the fluffiness, one delicious recipe at a time.

VANILLA MAPLE LATTE

SERVES 1

Cook time 10 minutes

250 ml (9 fl oz) milk
1 teaspoon vanilla extract
2–3 teaspoons maple syrup
1 teaspoon vanilla syrup
60 ml (2 fl oz) espresso
whipped cream, to serve (optional)

Pour the milk in a small saucepan, add the vanilla extract and the maple and vanilla syrups. Over a medium–low heat, gently whisk the milk and syrup mixture until thoroughly combined. Bring to just below simmering point, then remove from the heat and leave to stand.

Make the espresso and pour into a large mug.

Pour the prepared milk over the espresso and stir gently.

Top with whipped cream, if desired, and serve immediately.

CLASSIC
TREATS

CHOCOLATE CHIP PANCAKES

SERVES 4

Prep time 10 minutes
Cook time 15 minutes

125 g (4 oz) plain (all-purpose) flour
1 teaspoon baking powder
2 tablespoons granulated sugar
200 ml (7 fl oz) buttermilk
1 egg
75 g (2¾ oz) chocolate chips
1 tablespoon vegetable oil, for frying
whipped cream, to serve

Sift the flour and baking powder into a large bowl, add the sugar and make a well in the centre. Whisk together the buttermilk and egg in a jug, then gradually whisk into the flour mixture to form a smooth batter. Stir in the chocolate chips.

Heat the oil in a large frying pan over a medium heat and add tablespoons of the pancake batter, spaced well apart. Cook for 1–2 minutes until bubbles start to appear. Flip the pancakes over gently and cook for a further 1 minute until golden. Remove from the pan and keep warm. Repeat with the remaining batter.

Serve the pancakes with whipped cream.

CHOCOLATE PANCAKES WITH CHOCOLATE SAUCE

SERVES 4

Prep time 10 minutes
Cook time 25 minutes

100 g (3½ oz) plain (all-purpose) flour
1 tablespoon cocoa powder
pinch of salt
2 eggs, beaten
300 ml (½ pint) milk
2 tablespoons unsalted butter, melted
knob of butter, for frying
225 g (7½ oz) shop-bought red fruit compote

For the sauce

174 g (6 oz) milk chocolate, broken into small pieces
50 g (2 oz) unsalted butter
2 tablespoons golden syrup
100 ml (3½ fl oz) milk

Sift the flour, cocoa powder and salt into a large bowl and make a well in the centre. Pour the eggs into the well, then gradually whisk into the flour mixture. Add the milk a little at a time, whisking to make a smooth batter. Stir in the melted butter. Set aside.

To make the sauce, gently melt the chocolate, butter and golden syrup in a saucepan over a low heat. Stir in the milk and heat through for 2–3 minutes until the sauce thickens, stirring frequently. Keep warm.

Heat a little of the butter for frying in an 18 cm (7 inch) nonstick frying pan. Add a ladleful of the batter and tilt the pan to coat the base. Cook for 1–2 minutes until golden and then flip the pancake over to cook the other side for a further 1 minute. Remove from the pan and keep warm. Repeat with the remaining batter to make 8 pancakes, adding more butter if necessary.

To serve, fill each pancake with a little of the compote and drizzle with the chocolate sauce.

BUTTERMILK PANCAKES WITH BACON & MAPLE SYRUP

SERVES 4

Prep time 15 minutes
Cook time 15 minutes

1 egg
165 ml (6 fl oz) buttermilk
15 g (½ oz) butter, melted
50g (2 oz) plain (all-purpose) flour
25 g (1 oz) fine cornmeal
1 teaspoon bicarbonate of soda
1 tablespoon vegetable oil, for frying
8 unsmoked streaky bacon rashers
maple syrup, to serve

In a large bowl, whisk together the egg, buttermilk and melted butter. Sift in the flour, cornmeal and bicarbonate of soda and mix together gently – do not overmix.

Heat the oil in a large frying pan over a medium heat and add 3 tablespoons of the pancake batter, spaced well apart. Cook for 2–3 minutes until bubbles start to appear. Flip the pancakes over gently and cook for a further 1–2 minutes. Remove from the pan and keep warm. Repeat with the remaining batter to make 12 pancakes.

Meanwhile, cook the bacon under a preheated hot grill (broiler) for 3–4 minutes on each side until crisp.

Serve the pancakes in stacks of 3 topped with bacon rashers and drizzled with maple syrup.

BLUEBERRY PANCAKES

SERVES 4

Prep time 10 minutes
Cook time 15 minutes

250 ml (8 fl oz) milk
2 eggs
100 g (3½ oz) caster (superfine) sugar
75 g (3 oz) butter, melted, plus extra for frying
1 teaspoon baking powder
pinch of salt
250g (8 oz) plain (all-purpose) flour
100 g (3½ oz) blueberries, plus extra to serve
runny honey, to serve

Whisk together the milk, eggs, sugar and melted butter in a large bowl. Whisk in the baking powder and salt, add half the flour and whisk well until all the ingredients are incorporated, then whisk in the remaining flour. Add the blueberries and mix well.

Heat a large nonstick frying pan over a medium heat. Using a scrunched-up piece of kitchen paper, dip into the extra melted butter and use to wipe the pan. Spoon in large tablespoons of the batter, spaced well apart. Add extra butter for frying if needed.

Cook for 1–2 minutes on each side, or until golden brown. Remove from the pan and keep warm. Repeat until all the batter is used.

Serve the pancakes with extra blueberries and a little honey drizzled over.

CRÊPES SUZETTE

SERVES 4

Prep time 15 minutes
Cook time 35 minutes

100 g (3½ oz) plain (all-purpose) flour
pinch of salt
2 eggs, beaten
300 ml (½ pint) milk
2 tablespoons unsalted butter, melted, plus extra for frying

For the syrup

100 g (3½ oz) unsalted butter, softened
100 g (3½ oz) caster (superfine) sugar
grated zest and juice of 1 orange
4 tablespoons orange liqueur
1 tablespoon brandy

Sift the flour and salt into a large bowl and make a well in the centre. Pour in the eggs, then gradually whisk into the flour. Gradually add the milk, whisking to form a smooth batter. Stir in the melted butter.

Heat a little butter in a 20 cm (8 inch) nonstick frying pan. Add a ladleful of batter, tilting the pan to coat the base. Cook for 1–2 minutes until golden, then flip and cook for a further minute. Remove from the pan and keep warm. Repeat with the remaining batter and extra butter as needed to make 8 pancakes.

To make the syrup, place the butter and sugar in a bowl and whisk until creamy, then beat in the orange zest and juice and half the liqueur.

Place the mixture in a large frying pan and boil rapidly for 2 minutes. Reduce the heat and add the crêpes one at a time, folding each one in half and then into quarters in the syrup, until hot.

Warm the remaining orange liqueur and brandy in a small saucepan, carefully set alight and pour over the crêpes. Serve immediately.

BANANA BUTTERMILK PANCAKES

SERVES 4

Prep time 10 minutes
Cook time 15 minutes

125 g (4 oz) plain (all-purpose) flour
1 teaspoon baking powder
pinch of salt
200 ml (7 fl oz) buttermilk
1 egg
2 small bananas, thinly sliced
1 tablespoon vegetable oil, for frying

To serve
1 banana, sliced
25 g (1 oz) pecan nuts, chopped
1 tablespoon runny honey

Sift the flour, baking powder and salt into a large bowl and make a well in the centre. Whisk together the buttermilk and egg in a jug, then gradually whisk into the flour mixture to form a smooth batter. Carefully stir in the bananas.

Heat a large nonstick frying pan over a medium heat. Using a scrunched-up piece of kitchen paper, dip into the oil and use to wipe over the pan.

Drop 3 large tablespoons of the batter, spaced well apart, into the pan to make 3 pancakes, spreading the batter out slightly with a spoon. Cook for 2–3 minutes until bubbles start to appear and the underside is golden brown, then flip over and cook for a further 2 minutes. Remove from the pan and keep warm. Repeat to make 8 pancakes.

Serve the pancakes topped with sliced banana, sprinkled with pecans and drizzled with honey.

BANOFFEE PANCAKES

SERVES 4

Prep time 15 minutes, plus resting
Cook time 30 minutes

100 g (3½ oz) plain (all-purpose) flour
pinch of salt
1 egg
1 egg yolk
300 ml (½ pint) milk
2–3 tablespoons vegetable oil, for frying
2 bananas, sliced
150 ml (¼ pint) double (heavy) cream, whipped to soft peaks
2 tablespoons coarsely grated plain dark chocolate or 2 chocolate digestive biscuits, crushed

For the sauce
50 g (2 oz) unsalted butter
50 g (2 oz) light muscovado (brown) sugar
2 tablespoons golden syrup
150 ml (¼ pint) double (heavy) cream

Sift the flour into a large bowl, add the salt, egg and egg yolk, then gradually whisk in the milk to make a smooth batter. Set aside for 30 minutes.

To make the sauce, put the butter, sugar and golden syrup into a small saucepan and heat gently, stirring occasionally, until the butter has melted and the sugar dissolved. Bring to the boil and cook for 3–4 minutes until just beginning to darken around the edges.

Take the pan off the heat and gradually pour in the cream. Tilt the pan to mix and, as the bubbles subside, stir with a wooden spoon. Set aside.

Pour the oil for frying into a nonstick 18 cm (7 inch) frying pan, heat and then pour off the excess into a small bowl. Pour a quarter of the pancake batter into the pan and tilt to coat the base evenly. Cook for about 2 minutes until the underside is golden. Loosen with a palette knife, flip over and cook for another 2 minutes. Remove from the pan and keep warm. Repeat to make 4 pancakes, greasing the pan as needed.

Top one half of each pancake with banana slices, fold over and drizzle with toffee sauce.

Place a spoonful of the whipped cream on each pancake, then sprinkle over the grated chocolate or crushed biscuits.

SWEET &
STICKY
TREATS

SWEET ALMOND GRILLED PANCAKES

SERVES 4

Prep time 10 minutes
Cook time 30 minutes

125 g (4 oz) plain (all-purpose) flour
1 tablespoon caster (superfine) sugar
1 egg
300 ml (½ pint) milk
1 teaspoon vegetable oil, plus extra for frying
50 g (2 oz) flaked almonds

For the filling
50 g (2 oz) ground almonds
1 teaspoon vanilla extract
125 g (4 oz) icing (confectioners') sugar, plus 2 tablespoons extra for sprinkling
200 g (7 oz) mascarpone

To make the filling, mix all the ingredients in a bowl and set aside.

Sift the flour into a large bowl and add the caster sugar. Make a well in the centre. Beat the egg, milk and oil together in a jug, then gradually whisk into the flour mixture to form a smooth batter.

Heat a little oil in a large nonstick frying pan then add 2 tablespoons of the batter, tilting the pan so it covers the base evenly. Cook for 2 minutes until the underside is golden brown, then carefully flip over and cook for a further 1–2 minutes. Remove from the pan and keep warm. Repeat to make 8 pancakes.

Divide the filling between the pancakes, then fold over and arrange in a large ovenproof dish. Sprinkle over the flaked almonds and extra icing sugar. Cook under a preheated hot grill (broiler) for 3–4 minutes until warmed and lightly golden.

RAINBOW PANCAKE STACK

SERVES 4

Prep time 15 minutes
Cook time 15 minutes

200 g (7 oz) self-raising flour
1 teaspoon baking powder
2 tablespoons caster (superfine) sugar
200 ml (7 fl oz) milk
3 eggs
25 g (1 oz) unsalted butter, melted, plus extra for frying
green, blue, yellow and red gel food colouring

To serve
whipped cream
maple syrup

Place the flour, baking powder and sugar in a large bowl and make a well in the centre.

Mix the milk, eggs and melted butter in a jug and pour into the well. Gradually whisk into the flour mixture to form a smooth batter.

Divide the batter into 4 bowls. Add a little drop of food colouring to each until you reach the desired colour.

Melt a small knob of butter in a large nonstick frying pan. Add spoonfuls of batter, spaced well apart, into the pan and shape into 4–5cm (1½–2 inch) rounds. Cook for 2–3 minutes until bubbles appear on the surface, then flip over and cook for a further 30–60 seconds until slightly golden. Remove from the pan and keep warm. Repeat with the remaining batter and extra butter as needed.

Serve the pancakes in multicoloured stacks, topped with whipped cream and a drizzle of maple syrup.

RED VELVET PANCAKES

SERVES 4

Prep time 10 minutes
Cook time 15 minutes

125 g (4 oz) plain (all-purpose) flour
1 teaspoon baking powder
1 tablespoon cocoa powder
pinch of salt
1 tablespoon caster (superfine) sugar
200 ml (7 fl oz) buttermilk
1 teaspoon vanilla extract
1 egg
red gel food colouring
1 tablespoon vegetable oil, for frying

To serve

150 g (5½ oz) cream cheese, softened
3 tablespoons icing (confectioners') sugar
3 tablespoons milk
raspberries
strawberries

Sift the flour, baking powder, cocoa powder and salt into a large bowl and stir in the sugar. Make a well in the centre. Whisk together the buttermilk, vanilla extract and egg in a jug, then gradually whisk into the flour mixture to form a smooth batter.

Add a small amount of food colouring and mix well. Add more food colouring as needed until the batter is a dark red colour.

Heat a large nonstick frying pan over a medium heat. Using a scrunched-up piece of kitchen paper, dip into the oil and use to wipe over the pan.

Drop large tablespoons of the batter, spaced well apart, into the pan. Cook for 2–3 minutes until bubbles start to appear and the underside is golden brown, then flip over and cook for a further 2 minutes. Remove from the pan and keep warm. Repeat to use up the batter, adding more oil if needed.

Meanwhile, whisk the cream cheese, icing sugar and milk together in a bowl.

Serve the pancakes topped with a dollop of the cream cheese mixture and a scattering of raspberries and strawberries.

THICK SEMOLINA PANCAKES WITH HONEY

SERVES 4

Prep time 20 minutes
Cook time 8 minutes

225 g (7½ oz) plain (all-purpose) flour, plus extra for dusting
½ teaspoon salt
225 g (7½ oz) fine semolina
300 ml (½ pint) warm water
3 tablespoons melted ghee
4–5 tablespoons runny honey

Sift the flour and salt into a bowl and stir in the semolina. Gradually pour in the measured water and mix to form a soft dough. Knead well for about 5 minutes until smooth and pliable. Divide into 8 pieces and roll into ping pong-sized balls. Place on a lightly floured surface, cover with a clean, damp tea towel and leave to rest for 10 minutes.

Flatten and stretch each ball into a thin disc about 18 cm (7 inches) in diameter. Brush with melted ghee, then fold a third of the disc into the middle, the next third overlapping it, and the final third on top, so that you end up with a square parcel. Flatten each parcel and roll or stretch to about 15 cm (6 inches) square.

Heat a heavy-based griddle pan and brush with a little of the melted ghee. Then, add the pancakes in batches and cook, brushing with more ghee, for about 2 minutes on each side until browned.

Heat the honey in a small saucepan and drizzle over the pancakes. Serve for breakfast or as a hot snack.

HONEYED GRANOLA PANCAKES

SERVES 4

Prep time 10 minutes
Cook time 15 minutes

150 g (5½ oz) plain (all-purpose) flour
2 teaspoons baking powder
2 eggs
270 ml (9¼ fl oz) milk
3 tablespoons runny honey
200 g (7 oz) crunchy, granola-style cereal, lightly crushed
50 g (1¾ oz) butter

To serve
runny honey
Greek yogurt

Sift the flour and baking powder into a large bowl, then make a well in the centre. Whisk the eggs, milk and honey together in a jug and pour into the well. Whisk in the wet ingredients, gradually incorporating the flour, until you have a smooth batter. Stir in the granola.

Melt a pat of butter in a large nonstick frying pan and pour in small amounts of batter, spaced well apart, to make pancakes about 8 cm (3¼ inches) in diameter. Cook over a medium–low heat for 2–3 minutes until bubbles start to appear. Flip over and cook on the other side for another minute until golden. Remove from the pan and keep warm. Repeat with the remaining batter to make about 16 pancakes.

Serve the pancakes with honey drizzled over and a dollop of Greek yogurt.

LEMON & RICOTTA PANCAKE STACKS

SERVES 4

Prep time 15 minutes
Cook time 15 minutes

250 g (8 oz) ricotta cheese
125 ml (4 fl oz) milk
3 eggs, separated
grated zest and juice of 1 lemon
100 g (3½ oz) plain (all-purpose) flour
1 teaspoon baking powder
pinch of salt
3 tablespoons caster (superfine) sugar, plus extra for sprinkling
knob of unsalted butter, for frying

Place the ricotta, milk, egg yolks and lemon zest in a large bowl and beat together. Stir in the flour, baking powder, salt and sugar.

Whisk the egg whites in large clean bowl with an electric whisk until stiff, then gently fold into the ricotta mixture.

Heat a little of the butter in a large nonstick frying pan over a medium heat and add heaped dessertspoons of batter, spaced well apart, to form pancakes about 7 cm (3 inches) in diameter. Cook for 1–2 minutes on each side until golden brown. Remove from the pan and keep warm. Repeat with the remaining batter to make about 24 pancakes, adding a little more butter and reducing the heat if necessary.

Serve the pancakes in small stacks, drizzled with the lemon juice and sprinkled with extra caster sugar.

PANCAKES WITH WHITE CHOCOLATE & GINGER

SERVES 4

Prep time 30 minutes
Cook time 30 minutes

125 g (4 oz) plain (all-purpose) flour
2 tablespoons golden caster (superfine) sugar
1 egg
300 ml (½ pint) milk
vegetable oil, for frying

For the filling

1 piece stem ginger, about 15 g (½ oz), peeled and finely chopped
2 tablespoons caster (superfine) sugar, plus extra for sprinkling
250 g (8 oz) ricotta cheese
50 g (2 oz) raisins
150 g (5 oz) white chocolate, finely chopped
3 tablespoons double (heavy) cream

For the sauce

125 g (4 oz) caster (superfine) sugar
100 ml (3½ fl oz) water
200 g (7 oz) plain dark chocolate, broken into pieces
25 g (1 oz) butter

Sift the flour into a large bowl, then stir in the sugar. Make a well in the centre. Add the egg and a little milk, and whisk to make a stiff batter. Beat in the remaining milk.

Heat a little oil in an 18 cm (7 inch) nonstick frying pan until it starts to smoke. Pour off the excess and pour in a little batter, tilting the pan until the base is covered. Cook for 1–2 minutes until the underside starts to turn golden brown.

Loosen the edges and flip the pancake with a palette knife and cook for a further 30 seconds on the other side. Remove from the pan and repeat to make 4 pancakes.

To make the filling, mix all the ingredients together in a bowl. Place spoonfuls of the filling in the centre of the pancakes and fold them into quarters, enclosing the filling.

Place the pancakes in a lightly greased ovenproof dish and dust with sugar. Heat in a preheated oven. 200°C (400°F), Gas Mark 6, for 10 minutes.

Meanwhile, make the sauce. Place the sugar in a small saucepan with the water and stir until the sugar dissolves, then boil rapidly for 1 minute. Remove from the heat and add the chocolate. Leave to melt, then stir in the butter. Serve poured over the hot pancakes.

GINGERBREAD PANCAKES WITH STEM GINGER SAUCE

SERVES 4

Prep time 10 minutes
Cook time 25 minutes

125 g (4 oz) plain (all-purpose) flour
1 tablespoon caster (superfine) sugar
1 teaspoon ground ginger
1 teaspoon ground cinnamon
1 egg
300 ml (½ pint) milk
1 teaspoon vegetable oil, plus extra for frying
zest of ½ lemon
soured cream, to serve

For the sauce

50 g (2 oz) butter
4 tablespoons double (heavy) cream
2 tablespoons soft dark brown sugar
15 g (½ oz) stem ginger, drained and finely chopped
2 tablespoons stem ginger syrup

Sift the flour into a large bowl and add the sugar and spices. Make a well in the centre. Beat the egg, milk, oil and lemon zest together in a jug, then slowly stir into the well. Mix until a smooth batter forms.

Heat a little oil in a large nonstick frying pan, then add 2 tablespoons of the batter, tilting the pan so it covers the base evenly. Cook for 2 minutes until the underside is golden brown, then carefully flip over and cook for a further 1–2 minutes. Remove from the pan and keep warm. Repeat to make 8 pancakes.

Meanwhile, make the sauce. Place all the ingredients in a small saucepan and warm over a low heat for 5–6 minutes, stirring occasionally, until the butter has melted and the sugar dissolved.

Serve the pancakes with the sauce poured over and a dollop of soured cream on the side.

IRISH CREAM, BANANA & CHOCOLATE PANCAKES

MAKES ABOUT 20

Prep time 10 minutes
Cook time 20 minutes

125 g (4 oz) self-raising flour
75 g (3 oz) wholemeal plain (all-purpose) flour
2 teaspoons baking powder
50 g (2 oz) soft light brown sugar
2 large eggs
125 ml (4 fl oz) milk
2 tablespoons Irish cream liqueur
2 small, ripe bananas, roughly mashed
50 g (2 oz) milk or plain dark chocolate chips
15 g (½ oz) butter
vegetable oil, for frying

To serve
vanilla ice cream
chocolate sauce **(*see* page 27)**

Sift the flours and baking powder into a large bowl, then stir in the sugar and make a well in the centre. Whisk together the eggs, milk and liqueur in a jug, then pour into the well. Whisk together, gradually incorporating the flour from the edges until the batter is smooth. Stir in the mashed bananas and chocolate chips.

Heat the butter and a little oil in a large nonstick frying pan. Add small ladlefuls of the batter, spaced well apart, and cook for 2–3 minutes until bubbles start to appear on the surface, then flip over and cook for a further 30–60 seconds until golden. Remove from the pan and keep warm. Repeat with the remaining batter to make about 20 small pancakes, adding more butter and oil to the pan if necessary.

Serve the pancakes with scoops of vanilla ice cream and drizzled with chocolate sauce.

DRUNKEN CHOCOLATE PANCAKES

SERVES 4

Prep time 1 minute
Cook time 4 minutes

125 g (4 oz) plain (all-purpose) flour
2 tablespoons caster (superfine) sugar
1 egg
300 ml (½ pint) milk
butter or vegetable oil, for frying
50 g (2 oz) plain dark chocolate, broken into squares

For the sauce

100 g (3½ oz) butter
100 g (3½ oz) light muscovado sugar
4 tablespoons Rubis Chocolate Velvet Ruby or other chocolate liqueur or port

Sift the flour into a bowl, then stir in the sugar. Add the egg and a little milk, and whisk to make a stiff batter. Beat in the remaining milk.

Heat a little butter or oil in an 18 cm (7 inch) heavy-based frying pan until it starts to smoke. Pour off the excess and add a little batter into the pan, tilting it until the base is coated in a thin layer. Cook for 1–2 minutes until the underside begins to turn golden.

Flip the pancake with a palette knife and cook for a further 30–45 seconds. Slide the pancake out of the pan and make the remaining pancakes, greasing the pan as necessary. Set the pancakes aside.

To make the sauce, melt the butter and sugar in a frying pan, then add the liqueur or port.

Divide the chocolate among the pancakes, then fold into halves, then quarters, and slide into the pan. Warm through for 2 minutes and serve each pancake drenched in sauce.

FRUITY
TREATS

BUCKWHEAT PANCAKES WITH FRUIT COMPOTE

SERVES 4

Prep time 10 minutes, plus chilling
Cook time 20 minutes

100 g (3½ oz) buckwheat flour, sifted
½ teaspoon ground cinnamon
1 large egg, beaten
150 ml (¼ pint) milk
2 teaspoons vegetable oil, for frying
4 tablespoons Greek yogurt, to serve

For the compote
2 dessert apples, peeled, cored and chopped
2 pears, peeled, cored and chopped
100 g (3½ oz) blueberries
zest and juice of 1 orange
2 tablespoons water

Place the flour and half the cinnamon in a large bowl and make a well in the centre. Gradually whisk in the egg and milk to make a smooth batter. Chill for 30 minutes.

Heat a little of the oil in a large nonstick frying pan and pour a ladleful of the batter into the pan, swirling it around to cover the base. Cook until bubbles appear on the surface, then loosen the edges and flip it over. Cook for a further minute until golden. Remove from the pan and keep warm. Repeat with the remaining oil and batter to make 8 pancakes.

Meanwhile, make the compote. Place all the ingredients in a small saucepan and simmer for 10 minutes until the fruit has softened. Keep warm.

Serve the pancakes with the compote and a dollop of Greek yogurt sprinkled with the remaining cinnamon.

WHOLEMEAL BLACKBERRY PANCAKES & ZESTY YOGURT

SERVES 4

Prep time 10 minutes
Cook time 25 minutes

150 g (5 oz) wholemeal plain (all-purpose) flour
50 g (2 oz) plain (all-purpose) flour
1 teaspoon baking powder
300 ml (½ pint) milk
1 egg
2 tablespoons runny honey
150 g (5 oz) blackberries, halved, plus extra to serve
25 g (1 oz) coconut oil

For the zesty yogurt

12 g (4 oz) Greek yogurt
juice and zest of ½ lime
handful of mint leaves, shredded
1 tablespoon runny honey

Mix all the zesty yogurt ingredients in a small bowl and set aside.

Sift the flours and baking powder into a large bowl, then make a well in the centre. Mix together the milk, egg and honey in a jug. Pour into the dry ingredients and whisk until mixed. Stir in the blackberries.

Heat a little of the oil in a large nonstick frying pan, then add 2 tablespoons of batter for each pancake, spaced well apart, to make 4 pancakes. Cook for 4–5 minutes until golden and bubbles start to appear, then flip over and cook on the other side for a further 2–3 minutes. Remove from the pan and keep warm. Repeat with the remaining batter to make about 12 pancakes.

Serve the pancakes with dollops of the yogurt and extra blackberries.

GLUTEN-FREE FRUIT-STUFFED PANCAKES

SERVES 4

Prep time 10 minutes
Cook time 20 minutes

115 g (3¼ oz) rice flour
1 teaspoon gluten-free baking powder
½ teaspoon ground cinnamon
1 egg
finely grated zest of 1 lemon
175 ml (6 fl oz) soya milk
3 tablespoons water
2–3 teaspoons vegetable oil, for frying
1 peach, stoned and chopped
100 g (3½ oz) blueberries
60 g (2½ oz) raspberries
¼ cantaloupe melon, deseeded and chopped
5–6 mint leaves, shredded
4 tablespoons runny honey
Greek yogurt, to serve

Place the flour, baking powder, cinnamon, egg, lemon zest, milk and water in a blender or food processor and blend together.

Heat half the oil in a large nonstick frying pan over a medium heat, pour over one-quarter of the batter and cook for 2–3 minutes, then flip the pancake over and cook for a further 1–2 minutes. Remove from the pan and keep warm. Repeat with the remaining batter to make 4 pancakes, adding more oil to the pan if needed.

Gently mix the fruit together. Spoon one-quarter of the fruit mixture into the centre of each pancake and sprinkle over mint. Fold the pancakes in half and place on a baking sheet. Drizzle over the honey and cook under a preheated hot grill (broiler) for 2–3 minutes. Serve with a dollop of Greek yogurt.

PANCAKES WITH STRAWBERRY & LIME CRUSH

SERVES 4

Prep time 10 minutes
Cook time 25minutes

125 g (4 oz) brown plain (all-purpose) flour
1 tablespoon caster (superfine) sugar
1 egg
300 ml (½ pint) milk
1 teaspoon vegetable oil, plus extra for frying

For the crush
zest and juice of 1 lime
150 g (5 oz) strawberries, plus extra, halved, to serve
2 teaspoons runny honey

To make the crush, add all the ingredients to a food processor and blend to a coarse purée. Set aside.

Sift the flour into a large bowl and add the sugar. Make a well in the centre. Beat the egg, milk and oil together in a jug, then slowly stir into the well. Mix until a smooth batter forms.

Heat a little oil in a large nonstick frying pan, then add 2 tablespoons of the batter, tilting the pan so it covers the base evenly. Cook for 2 minutes until the underside is golden brown, then carefully flip over and cook for a further 1–2 minutes. Remove from the pan and keep warm. Repeat to make 8 pancakes.

Serve the pancakes topped with the crush and scattered with halved strawberries.

LACY RASPBERRY PANCAKES

SERVES 4

Prep time 15 minutes
Cook time 20 minutes

2 eggs
150 g (5 oz) plain (all-purpose) flour
1 teaspoon caster (superfine) sugar
300 ml (½ pint) milk
15 g (½ oz) butter, melted
300 ml (½ pint) double (heavy) cream
3 teaspoons runny honey
250 g (8 oz) raspberries
vegetable oil, for frying
icing (confectioners') sugar, for dusting

Whisk the eggs, flour and sugar in a bowl until well combined, then whisk in the milk to form a smooth batter. Whisk in the melted butter, then set aside.

To make the raspberry cream, whip the cream very lightly until just beginning to peak. Fold in the honey and raspberries and chill while making the pancakes.

Heat a little oil in a 15 cm (6 inch) nonstick frying pan. Transfer the batter to a jug with a narrow spout, and pour a very thin stream of the batter, starting in the centre of the pan and continuing in continuous circles around, then across the pan to form a small web pattern. Cook for about 1 minute until set, then, using a spatula, flip the pancake over and cook for a further 30 seconds. Remove from the pan and keep warm. Repeat to make 8 pancakes.

Serve the pancakes topped with a little of the raspberry cream and dusted with icing sugar.

PEACH & CINNAMON PANCAKES

SERVES 4

Prep time 10 minutes
Cook time 25 minutes

3 small ripe peaches
1 teaspoon ground cinnamon
6 tablespoons maple syrup
125 g (4 oz) self-raising flour
2 tablespoons golden caster (superfine) sugar
1 egg
150 ml (¼ pint) milk
vegetable oil, for frying

Halve and stone the peaches. Roughly chop 1 peach and set aside, then cut the remaining 2 into wedges and toss with a small pinch of the cinnamon and all the maple syrup in a small bowl. Set aside.

Sift the flour and remaining cinnamon into a large bowl and add the sugar. Make a well in the centre. Beat the egg and milk together in a jug, then pour into the well. Mix quickly and as lightly as possible until you have a batter the consistency of thick cream. Stir in the chopped peach.

Lightly oil a large nonstick frying pan. Drop heaped tablespoons of the batter, spaced well apart, into the pan. Cook over a medium heat for 1–2 minutes until bubbles start to appear on the surface and the underside is golden brown, then flip over and cook for a further 1–2 minutes. Remove from the pan and keep warm. Repeat to make 8 pancakes.

Serve the pancakes with a large spoonful of the peach and maple syrup mixture on each.

PEAR & MASCARPONE PANCAKES

SERVES 4

Prep time 10 minutes
Cook time 30 minutes

125 g (4 oz) plain (all-purpose) flour, sifted
2 eggs, beaten
300 ml (½ pint) milk
25 g (1 oz) butter, melted, plus extra for frying
500 g (1 lb) mascarpone cheese
2 tablespoons Amaretto liqueur
3 ripe pears, peeled, cored and diced
4 tablespoons runny honey

Place the flour in a large bowl and make a well in the centre. Pour the eggs into the centre and start to whisk, bringing in the flour. Gradually add the milk, whisking constantly, until you have a batter the consistency of double (heavy) cream. Whisk in the melted butter.

Add a little melted butter to a large nonstick frying pan. Pour in a small amount of the batter, swirling it around to coat the base of the frying pan. Cook for 1–2 minutes, then flip over and cook for about 1 minute. Remove from the pan and keep warm. Repeat with the remaining batter to make 8 pancakes.

Meanwhile, whisk together the mascarpone and Amaretto in a bowl, then briefly fold in the pears and 2 tablespoons of the honey to make a rippled effect.

Divide the mixture between the pancakes, fold each one into quarters and place in an ovenproof dish. Drizzle with the remaining honey and heat under a preheated hot grill (broiler) for 1–2 minutes before serving.

PANCAKES WITH VANILLA CHERRIES

SERVES 4

Prep time 10 minutes, plus resting
Cook time 20 minutes

125 g (4 oz) plain (all-purpose) flour
1 egg
300 ml (½ pint) milk
1 tablespoon caster (superfine) sugar
250 g (8 oz) cherries, pitted and halved
2 tablespoons freshly squeezed orange juice
2 tablespoons vanilla sugar
vegetable oil, for frying
4 tablespoons crème fraîche, to serve

Place the flour, egg, milk and sugar in a food processor or blender and blend to a smooth batter. Set aside for 10 minutes.

Meanwhile, add the cherries, orange juice and vanilla sugar to a small saucepan and warm over a low heat for 10 minutes.

Heat a small nonstick frying pan over a medium heat and add a little vegetable oil. Pour a ladleful of batter into the pan and swirl around to coat the base thinly. Cook for 2 minutes, or until golden underneath, then loosen the edges and flip over. Cook for 30 seconds. Remove from the pan and keep warm. Repeat with the remaining batter to make 8 pancakes.

Fold 2 pancakes onto each plate and spoon over the vanilla cherries. Serve with a tablespoon of crème fraîche.

RICOTTA PANCAKES WITH ORANGES & FIGS

SERVES 4

Prep time 10 minutes
Cook time 20 minutes

100 ml (3½ fl oz) milk
250 g (8 oz) ricotta cheese
75 g (3 oz) plain (all-purpose) flour
½ teaspoon baking powder
2 eggs, separated
1 tablespoon caster (superfine) sugar
25 g (1 oz) butter
2 oranges
2 teaspoons runny honey
3 figs, quartered

Place the milk, ricotta, flour, baking powder, egg yolks and sugar in a food processor or blender and process until smooth.

Whisk the egg whites in a clean bowl until soft peaks form, then fold into the batter.

Melt the butter in a large nonstick frying pan, drop spoonfuls of the batter into the pan, spaced well apart, and cook for 2–3 minutes on each side until golden. Remove from the pan, keep warm and repeat until all the batter is used.

Peel and segment the oranges over a bowl to catch the juice. Place the juice and honey in a small saucepan and warm through.

Serve the pancakes with the orange segments and fig quarters and the juice and honey poured over.

CHOCOLATE APPLE PANCAKES

SERVES 4

Prep time 15 minutes
Cook time 15 minutes

125 g (4 oz) plain (all-purpose) flour
1 tablespoon caster (superfine) sugar
1 egg
300 ml (½ pint) milk
1 teaspoon vegetable oil, plus extra for frying
40 g (1½ oz) unsalted butter
3 dessert apples, cored and thickly sliced
2 large pinches of ground cinnamon
4 tablespoons shop-bought chocolate and hazelnut spread
icing (confectioners') sugar, sifted, for dusting

Sift the flour into a large bowl and add the sugar. Make a well in the centre. Beat the egg, milk and oil together in a jug, then slowly stir into the well. Mix until a smooth batter forms. Set aside.

Heat a little oil in a 20 cm (8 inch) nonstick frying pan, then add one-quarter of the batter, tilting the pan so it covers the base evenly. Cook for 2 minutes until the underside is golden brown, then carefully flip over and cook for a further 1–2 minutes. Remove from the pan and keep warm. Repeat to make 4 pancakes.

Meanwhile, melt the butter in a separate large frying pan, then add the apples and fry for 3–4 minutes, stirring and turning until hot and lightly browned. Sprinkle over the cinnamon and keep warm.

Spread the pancakes with the chocolate spread, spoon the apples onto one half of each pancake and fold over. Dust with icing sugar and serve.

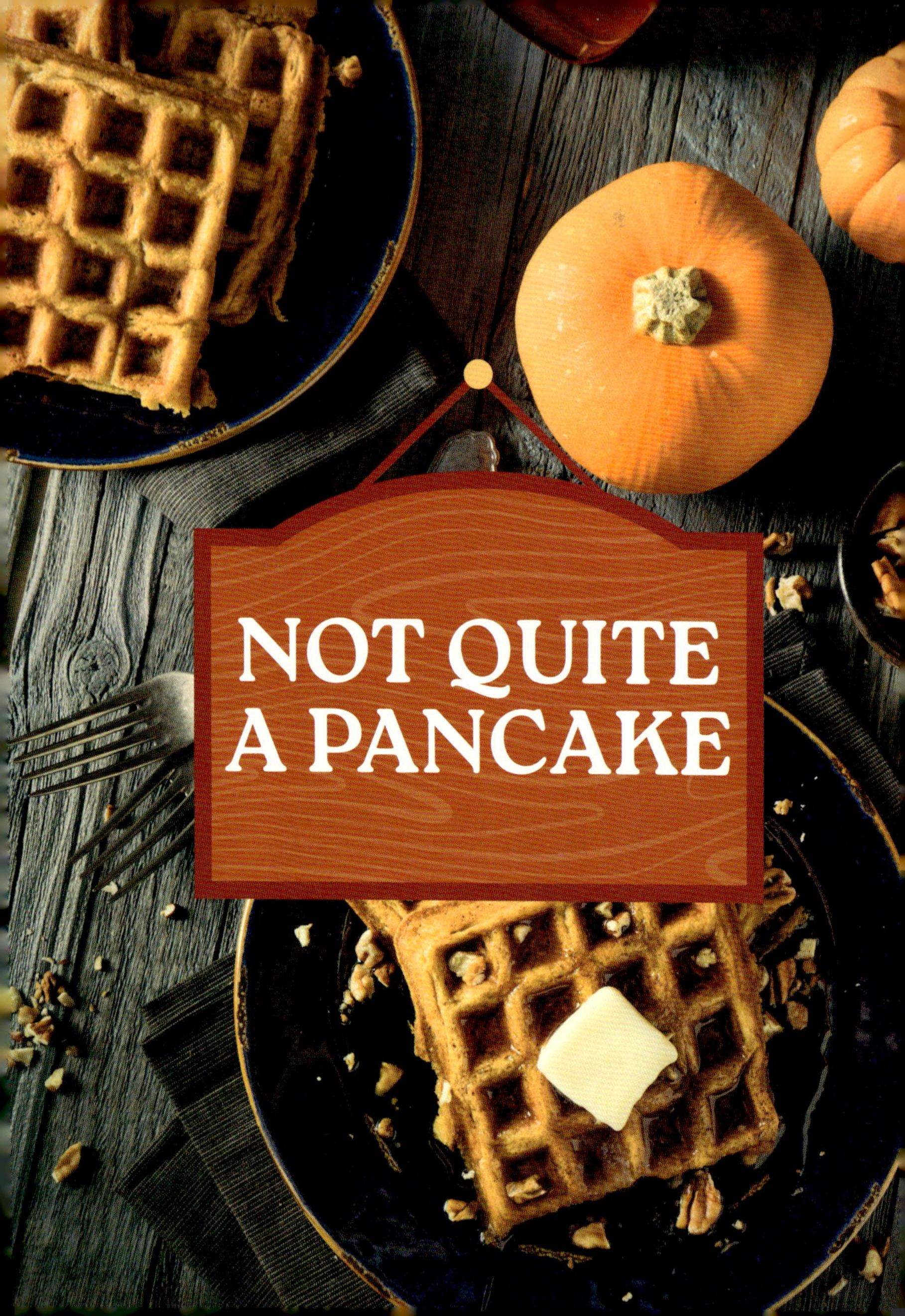
NOT QUITE
A PANCAKE

TRADITIONAL WELSH CAKES

MAKES 14–16

Prep time 15 minutes
Cook time 15 minutes

225 g (7½ oz) self-raising flour, plus extra for dusting
½ teaspoon mixed spice (pie spice mix)
100 g (3½ oz) unsalted butter, softened, plus extra for frying
pinch of salt
50 g (2 oz) caster (superfine) sugar, plus extra for sprinkling
75 g (3 oz) currants
1 large egg, lightly beaten
2 tablespoons runny honey

Sift the flour and mixed spice into a large bowl. Add the butter and rub in with your fingertips until the mixture resembles fine breadcrumbs, then stir in the salt, sugar and currants. Add the egg and honey and mix to form a soft but not sticky dough.

Turn the dough onto a floured surface and roll out to 5 mm (¼ inch) thick, then stamp out 14–16 rounds using a 7 cm (3 inch) plain cutter.

Heat a knob of butter in a large heavy-based frying pan. Add the rounds and cook over a low heat for 2–3 minutes, then flip over and cook for a further 2–3 minutes until risen and golden brown. Repeat with the remaining rounds, adding a little more butter to the pan, if necessary.

Serve warm, sprinkled with extra sugar.

FRUITED GRIDDLE CAKES

MAKES 30

Prep time 25 minutes
Cook time 18 minutes

250 g (8 oz) self-raising flour
125 g (4 oz) butter, diced, plus extra for spreading (optional)
100 g (3½ oz) caster (superfine) sugar, plus extra for sprinkling
50 g (2 oz) currants
50 g (2 oz) sultanas
1 teaspoon ground mixed spice
grated rind of ½ lemon
1 egg, beaten
1 tablespoon milk, if needed
oil, for greasing

Put the flour in a mixing bowl or a food processor. Add the butter and rub in with your fingertips or process until the mixture resembles fine breadcrumbs. Stir in the sugar, dried fruit, spice and lemon rind.

Add the egg, then gradually mix in milk, if needed, to make a smooth dough. Knead lightly, then roll out onto a lightly floured surface to 5 mm (¼ inch) thick. Stamp out 5 cm (2 inch) circles using a fluted biscuit cutter. Reknead the trimmings and continue rolling and stamping out until all the dough has been used.

Using a scrunched-up piece of kitchen paper, dip into the oil and use to wipe over a griddle or heavy-based nonstick frying pan. Heat the pan, then add the cakes in batches, regreasing the griddle or pan as needed, and fry over a low–medium heat for about 3 minutes on each side until golden brown and cooked through. Serve warm, sprinkled with a little extra sugar or spread with butter, if desired. Store in an airtight tin for up to 2 days.

SPICED DROP SCONES

SERVES 4

Prep time 10 minutes
Cook time 20 minutes

250 g (8 oz) self-raising flour
1 teaspoon ground cinnamon
1 teaspoon allspice
50 g (2 oz) golden caster (superfine) sugar
1 egg, beaten
300 ml (½ pint) milk
vegetable oil, for frying

To serve

vanilla ice cream
chocolate sauce (*see* **page 27**)

Add the flour, cinnamon, allspice and sugar to a large bowl and make a well in the centre. Pour the egg into the well and gradually add the milk, beating well until smooth.

Heat a little oil in a large nonstick frying pan over a medium heat. Drop large tablespoons of the batter into the pan, spaced well apart, and cook for 1–2 minutes until bubbles start to appear on the surface and the underneath is golden brown, then flip over and cook for a further 1–2 minutes. Remove from the pan and keep warm. Repeat with the remaining batter, adding more oil to the pan if necessary.

Serve the drop scones with scoops of vanilla ice cream and with chocolate sauce drizzled over.

BANANA & SULTANA DROP SCONES

SERVES 4

Prep time 10 minutes
Cook time 20 minutes

135 g (4 oz) self-raising flour
2 tablespoons caster (superfine) sugar
½ teaspoon baking powder
1 small banana, roughly mashed
1 egg, beaten
150 ml (¼ pint) milk
50 g (2 oz) sultanas
vegetable oil, for frying
butter, runny honey or maple syrup, to serve

Put the flour, sugar and baking powder in a large bowl. Add the mashed banana and egg. Whisk in the milk with a fork until you have a smooth, thick batter. Stir in the sultanas.

Heat a large nonstick frying pan over a medium heat. Using a scrunched-up piece of kitchen paper, dip into the oil and use to wipe over the pan. Drop heaped dessertspoons of the batter into the pan, spaced well apart. Cook for 2 minutes until bubbles appear on the surface and the undersides are golden. Flip over and cook for a further 1–2 minutes. Remove from the pan and keep warm. Repeat, adding more oil if needed, until all the batter is used.

Serve the drop scones topped with butter, honey or maple syrup.

TIPSY BERRY WAFFLES

SERVES 4

Prep time 15 minutes
Cook time 10 minutes

125 g (4 oz) plain (all-purpose) flour
1 teaspoon baking powder
pinch of salt
2 eggs
150 ml (¼ pint) milk
40 g (1½ oz) butter, melted and cooled
vegetable oil, for greasing (optional)
4 tablespoons crème fraîche, to serve

For the tipsy berries

15 g (½ oz) butter
250 g (8 oz) mixed berries, such as blueberries, blackberries and raspberries
1 tablespoon caster (superfine) sugar
2 tablespoons kirsch

Sift the flour, baking powder and salt into a large bowl. Make a well in the centre. Whisk together the eggs and milk in a jug and gradually beat into the dry ingredients until the batter is smooth and thick. Beat in the melted and cooled butter.

Heat a waffle iron and oil it if needed, according to the manufacturer's instructions. Spoon in enough batter to give a good coating, close and cook for 1 minute on each side until golden brown. Lift the lid, remove the waffle and keep warm. Repeat with the remaining batter to make 4 waffles.

Meanwhile, make the tipsy berries. Melt the butter in a nonstick frying pan, add the berries, sugar and kirsch and cook over a high heat, stirring gently, for 1–2 minutes.

Serve the waffles with the berries spooned over and a tablespoon of the crème fraîche.

WHITE CHOCOLATE & APRICOT WAFFLES

SERVES 4

Prep time 15 minutes
Cook time 10 minutes

125 g (4 oz) plain all-purpose) flour
1 teaspoon baking powder
pinch of salt
2 eggs
150 ml (¼ pint) milk
40 g (1½ oz) butter, melted and cooled
vegetable oil, for greasing (optional)

For the topping
300 ml (½ pint) single (light) cream
225 g 8 oz white chocolate, finely chopped
400g (14 oz) can apricot halves in juice, drained and sliced
pistachio nuts, crushed

Sift the flour, baking powder and salt into a large bowl. Make a well in the centre. Whisk together the eggs and milk in a jug, then gradually beat into the dry ingredients until the batter is smooth and thick. Beat in the melted and cooled butter.

Heat a waffle iron and oil it if needed, according to the manufacturer's instructions. Spoon in enough batter to give a good coating, close and cook for 1 minute on each side until golden brown. Lift the lid, remove the waffle and keep warm. Repeat with the remaining batter to make 4 waffles.

Meanwhile, make the topping. Pour the cream into a small saucepan and heat until hot, but not boiling. Place the chocolate in a heatproof bowl. Pour the hot cream over the chocolate and stir until the chocolate has melted and the mixture is smooth.

Pour the chocolate sauce over the waffles and top with apricot slices, then sprinkle over a few crushed pistachio nuts.

CHOCOLATE CINNAMON FRENCH TOAST

SERVES 2

Prep time 5 minutes
Cook time 5 minutes

2 eggs, lightly beaten
2 thick slices of seeded brown bread, cut in half
15 g (½ oz) butter
2 tablespoons golden caster (superfine) sugar
2 teaspoons cocoa powder
½ teaspoon ground cinnamon

Place the eggs in a shallow dish. Press the bread into the eggs, turning well to coat.

Melt the butter in a large nonstick frying pan and add the egg-soaked bread. Cook for about 3 minutes, turning as needed.

Meanwhile, mix the sugar, cocoa powder and cinnamon on a plate. Place the hot French toast on top, turning to coat in the mixture. Serve immediately.

FRENCH TOAST WITH BLUEBERRIES & REDCURRANTS

SERVES 4

Prep time 5 minutes
Cook time 15 minutes

3 eggs
100 ml (3½ fl oz) milk
50 ml (2 fl oz) double (heavy) cream
100 g (3½ oz) caster (superfine) sugar
2 teaspoons ground cinnamon
6 slices of thick white bread
400 g (13 oz) mixed blueberries and redcurrants
2 tablespoons water
75 g (3 oz) butter
crème fraîche, to serve

In a large bowl, whisk together the eggs, milk, cream, half the sugar and a pinch of the cinnamon.

Press the bread in the egg mixture and soak for a few minutes.

In a frying pan, combine the remaining cinnamon with the remaining sugar and toss the berries in the mixture until they are well coated. Add the water and cook the mixture over a medium heat for 3–4 minutes. Remove from the heat and keep warm.

In a separate large nonstick frying pan, melt half the butter. Carefully drain 3 slices of bread and fry for 2–3 minutes on each side, or until golden brown. Remove from the pan and keep warm. Repeat with the remaining butter and slices of bread. Drain the toast on kitchen paper and cut each slice in half diagonally.

Serve with the berry mixture and a dollop of crème fraîche.

GINGER SYRUP PAIN PERDU

SERVES 4

Prep time 5 minutes
Cook time 10 minutes

50 g (2 oz) salted butter
4 tablespoons double (heavy) cream
2 tablespoons soft dark brown sugar
15 g (½ oz) stem ginger, drained and finely chopped
2 tablespoons stem ginger syrup
2 eggs
100 g (3½ oz) caster (superfine) sugar
250 ml (8 fl oz) milk
4 slices of brioche bread, slightly stale
75 g (3 oz) unsalted butter

To serve
vanilla ice cream
icing (confectioners') sugar

Place the salted butter in a small pan with the cream, dark brown sugar, stem ginger and syrup. Warm over a low heat for 5–6 minutes, stirring occasionally, until the butter has melted and the sugar dissolved.

Meanwhile, place the eggs in a large, shallow bowl with the caster sugar and milk and whisk until smooth. Dip the brioche into the mixture, turning to coat both sides. Melt the unsalted butter in a large, nonstick frying pan and cook the brioche over a low–medium heat for 4–5 minutes, turning once, until golden.

Arrange on plates and top with a scoop of vanilla ice cream, a dusting of icing sugar and a drizzle of the ginger syrup.

RASPBERRY RIPPLE PAIN PERDU

SERVES 4

Prep time 5 minutes
Cook time 15 minutes

325 g (11 oz) frozen raspberries
1 teaspoon lemon juice
2 tablespoons icing (confectioners') sugar, plus extra for dusting
2 eggs
125 g (4 oz) caster (superfine) sugar
1 teaspoon vanilla extract (optional)
250 ml (8 fl oz) milk
4 thick slices of day-old farmhouse bread or brioche
75 g (3 oz) butter
crème fraîche, to serve (optional)

Place the raspberries in a saucepan with the lemon juice and icing sugar, and warm very gently until just beginning to collapse. Blend in a food processor until smooth, then pass through a sieve to remove the seeds.

Whisk together the eggs, caster sugar and vanilla extract (if using). Add the milk slowly, whisking until smooth and incorporated.

Dip the slices of bread in the egg mixture so that both sides are well coated. Melt the butter in a large nonstick frying pan and cook the coated bread slices gently for about 2 minutes on each side until crisp and golden.

Remove the bread from the pan and arrange on serving plates. Drizzle with the warm raspberry coulis to create a ripple effect, then dust with icing sugar and serve immediately with crème fraîche, if desired.

BANANA FRITTERS

SERVES 4

Prep time 20 minutes, plus standing
Cook time 5 minutes

225 g (7½ oz) plain (all-purpose) flour
½ teaspoon ground nutmeg
2 teaspoons ground cinnamon
375 ml (13 fl oz) sparkling water
sunflower oil, for deep-frying
4 bananas, halved both lengthways and widthways
3 tablespoons demerara sugar
1 tablespoon caster (superfine) sugar

Mix the flour, nutmeg and 1 teaspoon of the cinnamon together in a bowl, then make a well in the centre. Gradually whisk in enough of the sparkling water to make a smooth batter thick enough to coat the back of a spoon. Leave to stand for 20 minutes.

Fill a deep-sided saucepan one-third full with oil and heat to 180–190°C (350–375°F), or until a cube of bread browns in 30 seconds. Using a pair of tongs, dip the banana pieces, in batches, into the batter, then gently lower into the hot oil and cook for 30 seconds–1 minute until golden and crisp, taking care not to overcrowd the pan with too many at a time, as they will stick together and the oil temperature will drop. Remove from the pan with a slotted spoon and drain on kitchen paper.

Mix the sugars with the remaining cinnamon, then scatter over the hot fritters and serve immediately.

APPLE FRITTERS

SERVES 4–6

Prep time 10 minutes
Cook time 20 minutes

3 apples, peeled and cored
200 g (7 oz) plain (all-purpose) flour
1 teaspoon baking powder
1½ tablespoons caster (super-fine) sugar
1 teaspoon vanilla extract (optional)
200 ml (7 fl oz) milk
vegetable oil, for deep-frying
2 tablespoons icing (confectioners') sugar

Slice the apples into 1 cm (½ inch) thick rings and set aside.

Whisk the flour, baking powder and sugar in a bowl. Slowly add the vanilla (if using), and milk and whisk until you have a smooth batter.

Bring the oil to 170°C (340°F) in a deep saucepan. If you don't have a thermometer, throw in a drop of batter: it should sizzle, but not turn golden immediately. Dip the apple slices into the batter, coating well, then gently lower into the oil (taking care to not burn yourself) and cook for 2–3 minutes until golden and puffy. You will need to cook them in batches of 3–4 at a time to avoid overcrowding the pan.

Remove from the pan with a slotted spoon and drain on kitchen paper. Sift the icing sugar over the top and serve immediately.

CHURROS

MAKES 12

Prep time 20 minutes, plus cooling
Cook time 10 minutes

200 g (7 oz) plain (all-purpose) flour
¼ teaspoon salt
5 tablespoons caster (superfine) sugar
275 ml (9 fl oz) water
1 egg, beaten, plus 1 egg yolk
1 teaspoon vanilla extract
1 litre (1¾ pints) sunflower oil
1 teaspoon ground cinnamon

Mix the flour, salt and 1 tablespoon of the sugar in a bowl. Pour the water into a saucepan and bring to the boil. Remove from the heat, add the flour mixture and beat well. Return to the heat and stir until the mixture forms a smooth ball that leaves the sides of the pan almost clean. Remove from the heat and leave to cool for 10 minutes.

Gradually beat the whole egg, egg yolk and vanilla extract into the flour mixture until smooth. Spoon into a large piping bag fitted with a 1 cm (½ inch) star-shaped nozzle.

Pour the oil into a large saucepan to a depth of 2.5 cm (1 inch). Heat to 170°C (340°F). If you don't have a thermometer, pipe a tiny amount of the mixture into the oil: if the oil bubbles instantly, it is hot enough.

Pipe coils, S-shapes and squiggly lines into the oil, in small batches, cutting off the ends at the nozzle with kitchen scissors. Cook the churros for 2–3 minutes until they float and are golden, turn if needed.

Lift the churros out of the oil with a slotted spoon, drain on kitchen paper, then sprinkle with the remaining sugar mixed with the cinnamon. Continue piping and frying until all the mixture has been used. Serve warm or cold.

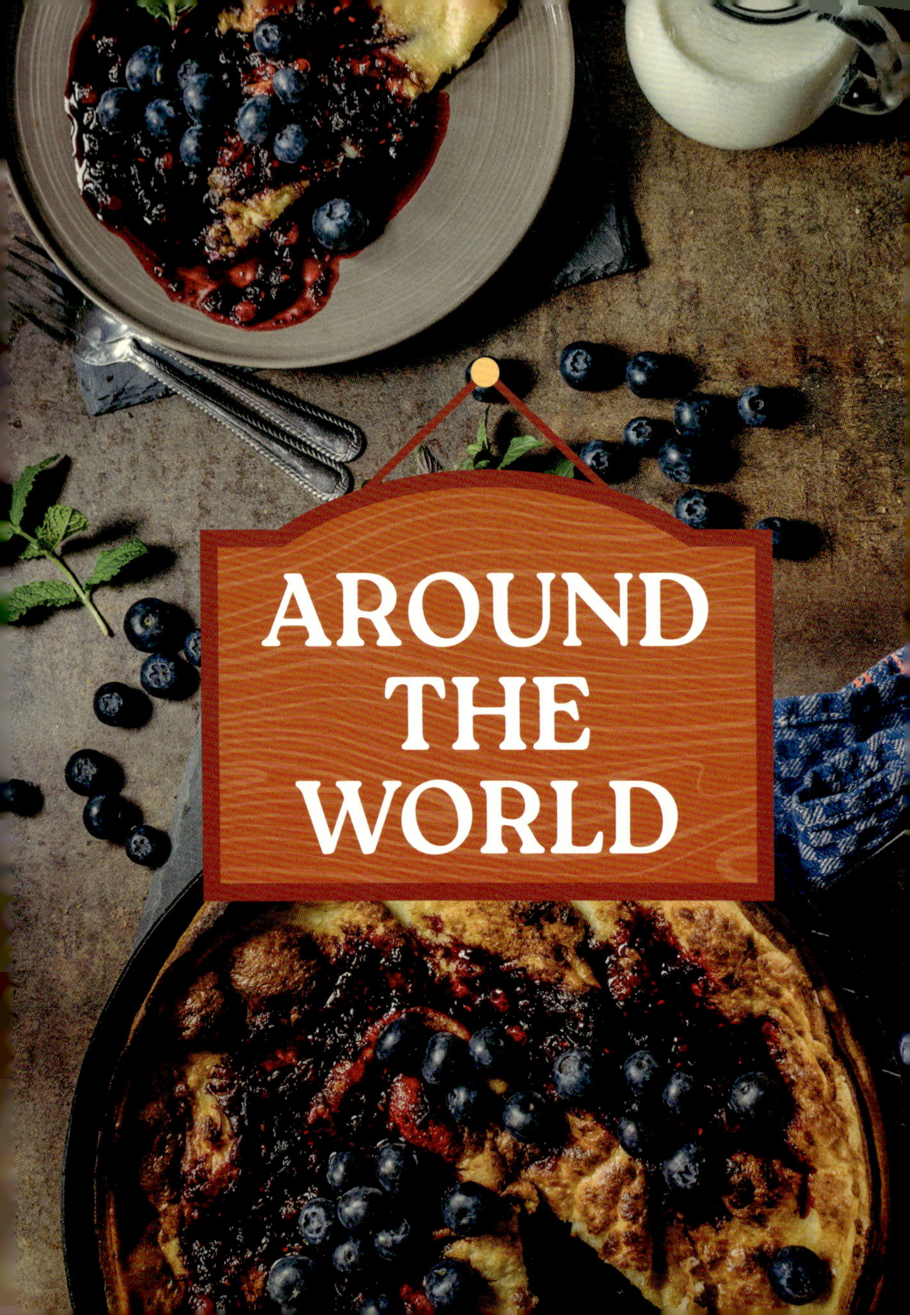
AROUND
THE
WORLD

DUTCH BABY PANCAKE

SERVES 4

Prep time 10 minutes
Cook time 20 minutes

100 g (3½ oz) plain (all-purpose) flour
2 tablespoons caster (superfine) sugar
150 ml (¼ pint) milk
1 teaspoon vanilla extract
3 large eggs
25 g (1 oz) unsalted butter
icing (confectioners') sugar, for dusting

To serve (optional)
mixed berries
whipped cream
maple syrup

Preheat the oven to 220°C (425°F), Gas Mark 7 and place a 25 cm (10 inch) ovenproof frying pan on the middle rack to warm while you make the batter. If you can, remove the shelf above as the Dutch baby will puff up.

Add the flour, sugar, milk, vanilla extract and eggs to a blender and blend until you have a smooth batter. Alternatively, add the flour to a large bowl, make a well in the centre, crack in the eggs, then add the milk and vanilla extract. Use a large whisk to beat the eggs into the milk, slowly incorporating the flour, until you have a smooth batter. Set aside.

Remove the frying pan from the oven and add the butter. Carefully swirl around to melt it and coat the bottom and sides of the pan. Quickly pour in the batter and return the pan to the oven.

Bake for 15–20 minutes until puffed up and golden. Remove from the oven, dust with a little icing sugar and serve immediately with the toppings of your choice.

PANNUKAKKU

SERVES 6

Prep time 10 minutes, plus standing
Cook time 40 minutes

150 g (5½ oz) plain (all-purpose) flour
1 teaspoon baking powder
pinch of salt
2 tablespoons caster (superfine) sugar
4 eggs
1 teaspoon vanilla extract
600 ml (1 pint) milk
25 g (1 oz) butter

To serve
icing (confectioners') sugar
raspberries or blueberries

Sift the flour, baking powder and salt into a large bowl, then stir in the sugar. Make a well in the centre. Mix the eggs, vanilla extract and milk in jug. Pour into the well and whisk, gradually working in the flour until it forms a thick batter. Set aside for 30 minutes.

Preheat the oven to 200°C (400°F), Gas mark 6. Melt the butter in a 23 x 30 cm (9 x 13 inch) baking dish, until it is sizzling. Carefully swirl to coat the baking dish with the butter, then pour in the batter.

Bake for 30–35 minutes, or until well risen and starting to turn golden brown.

Cut into squares and serve immediately dusted with icing sugar and with a handful of berries.

KAISERSCHMARRN

SERVES 4

Prep time 15 minutes, plus soaking
Cook time 20 minutes

25 g (1 oz) raisins
75 ml (5 tablespoons) rum
250 g (9 oz) plain (all-purpose) flour
pinch of salt
4 tablespoons caster (superfine) sugar
5 large eggs, separated
1 teaspoon vanilla extract
350 ml (12 fl oz) milk
50 g (1¾ oz) unsalted butter
icing (confectioners') sugar, to serve

Add the raisins and rum to a small saucepan and heat gently for 5 minutes over a low heat. Remove from the heat and set aside to soak for about 30 minutes.

Sift the flour and salt into a large bowl, then stir in 3 tablespoons of the caster sugar. Make a well in the centre. Mix the egg yolks, vanilla extract and milk in a jug. Whisk into the well, gradually bringing in all the flour to form a smooth batter.

Beat the egg whites in a clean bowl until stiff peaks form, then fold into the batter using a large metal spoon.

Melt half the butter in a large nonstick frying pan over a medium heat and, when foaming, pour in the batter. Cook for 3 minutes, then pour the rum and raisins evenly over the surface. Cook for a further 3–4 minutes, or until the pancake is golden brown underneath.

Cut into quarters with a spatula and carefully flip the quarters over. Cook for 3–4 minutes until golden brown on both sides.

Using 2 forks, tear the pancake into bite-size pieces. Add the remaining butter and caster sugar to the pan and toss the pancake pieces for 3–4 minutes until the sugar has caramelized.

Serve immediately, dusted with icing sugar.

HOTTEOK

MAKES 8

Prep time 30 minutes, plus standing
Cook time 20 minutes

2 teaspoons fast-action dried yeast
250 ml (9 fl oz) warm water
250 g (9 oz) plain (all-purpose flour), plus extra for dusting
½ teaspoon salt
2 tablespoons granulated sugar
1 tablespoon vegetable oil, plus extra for oiling and frying

For the filling

1 teaspoon ground cinnamon
2 tablespoons chopped walnuts
100 g (3½ oz) brown sugar

In a jug, stir together the yeast and water. Set aside for 5–10 minutes to activate the yeast. It is activated when bubbles form on the surface.

Sift the flour and salt into the bowl of a stand mixer fitted with a dough hook and stir in the sugar. Add the yeast mixture and oil. Knead until a smooth dough is formed. It should be sticky and stretchy.

Cover the bowl with clingfilm (plastic wrap) and set aside in warm place for 1 hour, or until doubled in size. Knead briefly to remove the air bubbles. Cover with clingfilm again and set aside in a warm place for 30 minutes.

Meanwhile, make the filling. Mix all the ingredients in a small bowl and set aside.

Turn the dough out onto a lightly floured surface and cut into 8 equal portions. With lightly oiled hands, flatten each into discs and divide the filling between each. Pull the edges of the dough together, pinching to seal into a ball shape.

Heat a little oil in a large nonstick frying pan over a medium heat. Put 1 ball, sealed-side down, in the pan, then flatten slightly with a spatula. Cook for 1 minute until golden brown underneath, then flip over. Press down for a few seconds to flatten again. Cook for a further 1 minute, or until golden brown on both sides. Remove from the pan and keep warm. Repeat to cook the remaining pancakes, adding more oil if needed. Serve warm.

TIGANITES

SERVES 4

Prep time 15 minutes, plus standing
Cook time 15 minutes

1 teaspoon fast-action dried yeast
475 ml (17 fl oz) lukewarm water
250 g (9 oz) plain (all-purpose) flour
½ teaspoon salt
2 teaspoons granulated sugar
vegetable oil, for frying

To serve
chopped walnuts
runny honey

Stir the yeast and water together in a jug, then set aside for 5–10 minutes for the yeast to activate. It is ready when bubbles form on the surface.

Sift the flour and salt into a large bowl and mix in the sugar. Pour in the yeast mixture and whisk until a smooth batter forms.

Cover with clingfilm (plastic wrap) and set aside for 20–30 minutes.

Heat about 1 cm (½ inch) of oil in a large nonstick frying pan over a medium heat. Drop in large spoonfuls of the batter, spaced well apart, and fry for 2–3 minutes on each side until golden brown. Remove from the pan, drain on kitchen paper and keep warm. Repeat until all the batter is used.

Serve the pancakes warm scattered with chopped walnuts and drizzled with honey.

CHOCOLATE BLINIS

MAKES ABOUT 28

Prep time 10 minutes
Cook time 20minutes

100 g (3½ oz) self-raising flour
15 g (½ oz) cocoa powder
½ teaspoon baking powder
1 tablespoon caster (superfine) sugar
1 egg, beaten
170 ml (5½ fl oz) milk
1 tablespoon vegetable oil, for frying
50 g (2 oz) milk chocolate, finely chopped

To serve
100 ml (3½ fl oz) crème fraîche
150 g (5 oz) raspberries

Sift the flour, cocoa powder and baking powder into a large bowl and stir in the sugar. Make a well in the centre and gradually whisk in the egg and a little of the milk to form a thick batter. Stir in the remaining milk.

Heat a large nonstick frying pan over a medium heat. Using a scrunched-up piece of kitchen paper, dip into the oil and use to wipe over the pan. Drop dessertspoons of the batter into the pan, spaced well apart.

Cook for 1 minute, then scatter a little of the chocolate over each. Cook for a further 1–2 minutes until bubbles start to appear on the surface and pop, then flip over and cook for a further 1–2 minutes until just firm. Remove from the pan and keep warm.

Repeat with the remaining batter to make about 28 blinis, adding more oil if necessary.

Serve the blinis topped with the crème fraîche and raspberries.

RASPBERRY & OATMEAL SCOTCH PANCAKES

MAKES 8

Prep time 10 minutes
Cook time 15 minutes

125 g (4 oz) self-raising flour
2 tablespoons golden caster (superfine) sugar
2 tablespoons oatmeal
1 egg
½ teaspoon vanilla extract
150 ml (¼ pint) milk
75 g (3 oz) raspberries, halved
vegetable oil, for frying
8 tablespoons maple syrup, to serve

Place the flour in a bowl with the sugar and oatmeal and stir well. Make a well in the centre.

Beat together the egg, vanilla extract and milk in a jug, then pour into the dry ingredients and beat lightly to make a batter with the consistency of thick cream. Carefully fold in the raspberries.

Add a little oil to a large nonstick frying pan. Drop tablespoons of the batter into the pan, spaced well apart, and cook over a medium heat for 1–2 minutes until bubbles rise to the surface and burst. Turn the pancakes over and cook for a further 1–2 minutes until golden and set. Remove from the pan and keep warm. Repeat with the remaining batter to make 8 pancakes, adding more oil if necessary.

Serve the pancakes with 1 tablespoon of maple syrup spooned over each.

WHOLEMEAL SULTANA PIKELETS

MAKES 18–20

Prep time 10 minutes
Cook time 15 minutes

75 g (3 oz) self-raising flour
75 g (3 oz) wholemeal self-raising flour
1 teaspoon baking powder
2 tablespoons soft light brown sugar
1 large egg
½ teaspoon vanilla extract
225 ml (7½ fl oz) buttermilk
50 g (2 oz) golden sultanas
1 small dessert apple, peeled, cored and coarsely grated (optional)
butter, for frying
warm maple syrup, to serve

Sift the flours and baking powder into a bowl, then stir in the sugar and make a well in the centre.

Whisk together the egg, vanilla extract and buttermilk in a jug, then pour into the well. Whisk together, gradually incorporating the flour from the edges until the batter is smooth and thick. Stir in the golden sultanas and grated apple (if using).

Heat a small knob of butter in a large nonstick frying pan, add tablespoons of the batter, spaced well apart, and cook for 1 minute until bubbles start to appear on the surface, then flip over and cook for a further 30–60 seconds until lightly golden. Remove from the pan and keep warm. Repeat to make 18–20 pikelets, adding a little more butter to the pan if necessary.

Serve the pikelets immediately, drizzled with warm maple syrup.

MOROCCAN PANCAKES

MAKES ABOUT 20

Prep time 20 minutes, plus resting
Cook time 20 minutes

500 g (1 lb) bread flour
150 g (5 oz) ground wheat or fine semolina
½ packet fast-action dried yeast
½ teaspoon salt
200 ml (7 fl oz) warm water
5 tablespoons groundnut (peanut) oil, plus extra for frying
100 g (3½ oz) butter, melted
granulated sugar or runny honey, to serve

Mix together all the dry ingredients in a large bowl, then add the water little by little, working it in until you have a very supple dough. Set aside to rest for 5 minutes.

Divide the dough into pieces the size of a tennis ball and place them on an oiled worktop. Leave to rest for a further 5 minutes.

Mix the oil and melted butter in a bowl. Coat your hands in the mixture and, taking each ball in turn, stretch the dough into a large, very thin, almost transparent, disc.

Coat your hands again in the butter and oil mixture, fold the discs in 3 – like a letter – you should have a narrow strip of dough, then into 3 again to form squares, tuck in the ends, and leave to rest for 10 minutes.

Cook each parcel in a hot frying pan for about 1 minute, turning over halfway through. Serve hot, with either sugar or honey.

SOUFFLÉ PANCAKES

SERVES 2

Prep time 10 minutes
Cook time 15 minutes

2 eggs, separated
1 teaspoon vanilla extract
2 tablespoons caster (superfine) sugar
3 tablespoons milk
50 g (1¾ oz) self-raising flour
vegetable oil, for frying

To serve
icing (confectioners') sugar
maple syrup

Add the egg yolks, vanilla extract and half the sugar to a bowl and whisk until pale and frothy. Gently fold in the milk and flour until just combined. Set aside.

Heat a large nonstick frying pan with a lid over a very low heat. Using a scrunched-up piece of kitchen paper, dip into the oil and use to wipe the pan. You only need a very light film of oil.

Meanwhile, add the egg whites with the remaining sugar to a clean bowl and whisk to form stiff peaks.

Gently fold the egg whites into the egg yolk mixture with a large metal spoon until fully incorporated, taking care to keep all the air in.

Using two-thirds of the mixture, drop 4 tall pancakes into the pan, spaced well apart. Cover with the lid and cook for 2–3 minutes. Remove the lid and add an additional scoop of batter onto each pancake. Cover again and cook for a further 4–5 minutes, or until the bases are light golden. Gently flip over, cover and cook for a further 4–5 minutes, or until golden brown on both sides and slightly firm to the touch.

Serve immediately with a dusting of icing sugar and drizzle of maple syrup.

INDEX

PUBLISHER'S NOTE

Standard level spoon measurements are used in all recipes.
1 tablespoon = one 15 ml spoon
1 teaspoon = one 5 ml spoon

Both imperial and metric measurements have been given in all recipes. Use one set of measurements only and not a mixture of both.

This book includes dishes made with nuts and nut derivatives. It is advisable for customers with known allergic reactions to nuts and nut derivatives, and those who may be potentially vulnerable to these allergies, such as babies and children with a family history of allergies, to avoid dishes made with nuts and nut oils. It is also prudent to check the labels of pre-prepared ingredients for the possible inclusion of nut derivatives.

Eggs should be medium unless otherwise stated. The Department of Health advises that eggs should not be consumed raw. This book contains dishes made with raw or lightly cooked eggs. It is prudent for more vulnerable people, such as pregnant and nursing mothers, the elderly, babies and young children, to avoid uncooked or lightly cooked dishes made with eggs. Once prepared, these dishes should be kept refrigerated and eaten promptly.

Milk should be whole (full fat) unless otherwise stated.

Ovens should be preheated to the specific temperature – if using a fan-assisted oven, follow manufacturer's instructions for adjusting the time and the temperature.

All microwave information is based on a 650-watt oven. Follow manufacturer's instructions for an oven with a different wattage.